BALAAM'S DONKEY TALES

5 Bedtime Stories of Talking Animals and Divine Messages

BLUME POTTER

INTRODUCTION

Welcome to Balaam's Donkey Tales: 5 Bedtime Stories of Talking Animals and Divine Messages, a special collection of Bible-inspired stories designed to spark your child's imagination while instilling timeless values. Each tale is narrated by Balaam's wise and faithful donkey, who takes young readers on a journey through moments of divine intervention, obedience, and the importance of being in tune with God's will.

These stories are more than just bedtime tales; they are gentle lessons wrapped in the warmth of storytelling. Perfect for cuddling up before bed, this book will captivate your child's heart and mind while teaching them the significance of listening to God's guidance, even when it comes in the most unexpected ways.

As you share these stories with your children or grandchildren, you'll not only be nurturing their spiritual growth but also creating cherished memories that will last a lifetime. Let the adventures of Balaam's talking donkey lead your little ones into peaceful, meaningful slumber, with hearts open to the wisdom and love found in God's Word.

This book is a must-have addition to your family's bedtime routine, ensuring that your children and grandchildren drift off to sleep with faith-filled stories that will guide them throughout their lives.

CHAPTER ONE:
THE WISE DONKEY

In a quiet corner of the countryside, where the sun's rays gently kissed the earth and the wind whispered through the trees, lived a donkey unlike any other. This donkey, Balaam's faithful companion, was known far and wide for his wisdom. He wasn't just any ordinary donkey—he was a thinker, always observing, always aware of the world around him.

Day after day, the donkey watched as Balaam, his master, went about his tasks. Balaam was a man of great knowledge, and many sought his advice. Yet, the donkey often sensed things that Balaam, for all his wisdom, overlooked.

One bright morning, Balaam approached the donkey with a new task. "We have a journey to take," Balaam said, as he placed a saddle on the donkey's back. The donkey's ears twitched, and he felt a stirring in his heart—a sense that something wasn't quite right.

As they set off on the dusty road, the donkey's senses were on high alert. The trees seemed to sway differently, the birds sang in hushed tones, and the path ahead felt heavy with an unseen weight. With every step, the donkey felt more certain that this was no ordinary journey.

Balaam, lost in his thoughts, didn't notice the subtle signs around him. But the donkey did. He slowed his pace, his ears perked up, and his eyes scanned the path ahead. Something was wrong, but what? The donkey didn't know yet, but he knew one thing for certain: they needed to be careful.

As they continued down the road, the donkey's heart beat faster. He knew that being in tune with God's will was important, even for a humble donkey like himself. And on this day, that wisdom would be put to the test.

With each step, the donkey carried not just Balaam, but also a sense of responsibility—to be aware, to listen, and to act when the time was right. Little did Balaam know, his wise donkey was already laying the groundwork for the extraordinary events that were about to unfold.

And so, they journeyed on, the wise donkey ever watchful, knowing that the signs were there for those who were willing to see them.

CHAPTER TWO:
THE INVISIBLE ANGEL

As Balaam rode his wise donkey down the familiar path, everything seemed normal to him. The sun still shone brightly, and the road stretched out ahead, just as it always did. But the donkey knew better. Something was different, something unseen yet deeply felt.

Suddenly, the donkey halted. Balaam, lost in his thoughts, frowned and urged the donkey forward, but the donkey refused to move. His eyes were wide with fear, his legs trembling as he stared ahead at the empty road. Except the road wasn't empty—not to the donkey. There, blocking their way, stood a mighty angel, shimmering with an unseen light, invisible to Balaam but clear as day to the donkey.

The donkey's heart raced. He knew the angel was a messenger from God, and he also knew that this was no ordinary moment. The angel's presence filled the air with a sense of awe and warning. But how could he make Balaam see what was so clear to him?

With great care, the donkey tried to step aside, hoping to avoid the angel's path. But Balaam, frustrated and unaware of the danger ahead, struck the donkey to make him move forward. The donkey, confused and afraid, tried to resist, understanding the importance of staying where they were.

The angel's gaze remained fixed on Balaam, yet it was the donkey who saw the danger, who understood the divine warning. The donkey's refusal to move wasn't stubbornness; it was a desperate attempt to protect his master from a peril he couldn't see.

Again, Balaam struck the donkey, his patience wearing thin. But the donkey, ever faithful, stood firm, his eyes still locked on the invisible angel. He knew the risks of disobeying his master, but the greater risk lay in ignoring the divine presence before him.

In this moment, the donkey's wisdom shone through. He recognized the spiritual reality that Balaam could not see, and he understood that sometimes, the warnings God gives are not always visible to the eye but must be felt with the heart.

The road ahead was filled with uncertainty, but the donkey's fear was not for himself; it was for Balaam, who was blind to the danger. The donkey's actions, though misunderstood, were a testament to his deep awareness of the divine, and his determination to heed the warning that Balaam could not perceive.

And so, they stood at an impasse, the wise donkey frozen in place, his heart pounding with the knowledge that sometimes, the most important signs are the ones we cannot see.

CHAPTER THREE:
THE TALKING DONKEY

Balaam's frustration grew with each passing moment. His once faithful donkey, who had always carried him without complaint, now refused to move forward. Balaam couldn't understand the sudden change. Angered by the donkey's apparent stubbornness, he struck the donkey again, urging it to continue down the road.

But instead of moving, the donkey did something extraordinary—something that Balaam could never have expected. The donkey turned its head, and in a calm and clear voice, it spoke.

"Why are you hitting me?" the donkey asked, its voice filled with sadness. "Have I not always served you faithfully? Have I ever done this to you before?"

Balaam froze in shock. His eyes widened, and for a moment, he could hardly believe what he was hearing. His donkey, an animal he had ridden countless times, was now speaking to him as if it were the most natural thing in the world.

Gathering his wits, Balaam responded, "You've made a fool of me! If I had a sword in my hand, I would kill you right now."

The donkey, ever patient and wise, replied, "Am I not your donkey, the one you have ridden all these years? Have I ever acted this way before?"

Balaam paused. The donkey's words made him think. No, the donkey had never acted this way before. In all the years they had traveled together, the donkey had been loyal and dependable. So why now? Why this sudden change?

And then, in that moment of reflection, Balaam began to realize that this was no ordinary event. This was something greater, something divine. The donkey's voice was not just an oddity; it was a sign, a direct communication from God.

Balaam's anger melted away, replaced by a deep sense of awe. He understood now that God was speaking to him in a way he had never imagined—through the mouth of a humble donkey. The very creature he had thought to punish was, in fact, delivering a message from the Almighty.

This unexpected conversation opened Balaam's eyes to the surprising ways in which God can communicate with us. Sometimes, the divine message comes in ways we least expect, and it is up to us to listen, even when the messenger is as unlikely as a talking donkey.

And so, Balaam listened, his heart now open to the divine intervention that had stopped him on his journey. He realized that God's voice could come through anyone or anything, and that it was his duty to pay attention, no matter how surprising the source.

CHAPTER FOUR:
THE ANGEL REVEALED

As Balaam stood in stunned silence, still reeling from the conversation with his donkey, the air around them began to shimmer. The donkey, who had seen what Balaam could not, now relaxed, sensing that the moment of truth had arrived.

Suddenly, the angel that had been hidden from Balaam's sight appeared before him. Tall and radiant, with a sword gleaming in its hand, the angel's presence was overwhelming. Balaam's eyes widened as he took in the sight of the divine messenger standing on the path. The reality of the situation hit him with full force.

The angel spoke with a voice that was both powerful and gentle, "Why have you struck your donkey these three times? I have come to oppose you because your path is a reckless one before me."

Balaam's heart sank as the weight of his actions became clear. He had been so focused on his own plans, so determined to push forward, that he had ignored the signs all around him—even the miraculous speech of his donkey. The truth was undeniable: he had gone astray, and his stubbornness had blinded him to the divine warning.

Falling to his knees, Balaam bowed his head in humility. "I have sinned," he confessed, his voice trembling. "I did not realize you were standing in the road to oppose me. If you are displeased, I will go back."

The angel regarded Balaam with a look of both sternness and compassion. "Go with the men," the angel instructed, "but speak only what I tell you."

The donkey, who had faithfully borne the burden of both the journey and the unseen danger, felt a deep sense of relief. The tension that had gripped him for so long began to ease, knowing that Balaam had finally seen the truth.

Balaam's heart was heavy with regret, but also filled with a new understanding. He realized the importance of humility, of being open to correction, and of recognizing when he had gone off course. The experience had taught him a powerful lesson: that even the wisest among us can be blind to the truth, and that it often takes a moment of divine revelation to bring us back to the right path.

And so, with a renewed sense of purpose, Balaam
continued on his journey, guided not just by his own will,
but by the will of the divine, ever mindful of the angel's
words and the wisdom of his faithful donkey.

CHAPTER FIVE:
THE PATH OF OBEDIENCE

With the angel's words still echoing in his mind, Balaam gently urged his donkey forward. The road ahead, once filled with uncertainty and unseen dangers, now seemed clear and purposeful. The donkey, who had faithfully carried Balaam through the trials of the journey, walked with a lightness in his step, proud to have played a part in God's plan.

As they continued on their way, Balaam was no longer the same man who had begun the journey. He was more cautious, more reflective, and most importantly, more obedient. The lessons he had learned from his wise donkey and the encounter with the angel had left a deep mark on his heart. He knew now that following God's path required not just wisdom, but also humility and a willingness to listen to guidance, no matter how unexpected the source.

The donkey, too, felt a sense of fulfillment. He had been used by God in a way he could never have imagined, and the thought filled him with pride. He understood now that even the smallest and humblest of creatures could play a significant role in God's plans.

Together, Balaam and his donkey journeyed on, their hearts aligned with the divine purpose that had been revealed to them. Balaam's steps were more measured, his decisions more thoughtful, as he sought to align his will with God's.

As the sun dipped low on the horizon, casting a golden glow over the path ahead, Balaam reflected on the journey they had taken. He knew that the road of obedience was not always easy, but it was the right path—the path that led to peace, purpose, and true understanding.

The story of Balaam and his talking donkey ended with a simple yet profound truth: that God's guidance can come in many forms, and it is up to us to be open, attentive, and willing to follow, no matter how unexpected the messenger may be.

And so, with a heart full of gratitude and a renewed sense of direction, Balaam continued down the path of obedience, trusting that God's guidance would always lead him true. The donkey, ever faithful, walked beside him, content in the knowledge that he had fulfilled his purpose, and that together, they had learned the true meaning of following God's will.